THE INDIANS OF MEXICO

A BOOK TO BEGIN ON

THE INDIANS OF MEXICO

By MARGARET C. FARQUHAR

Illustrated by Mel Klapholz

HOLT, RINEHART AND WINSTON

New York   Chicago   San Francisco

Copyright © 1967 by Margaret C. Farquhar : Illustrations Copyright ©
1967 by Mel Klapholz : All rights reserved, including the right to repro-
duce this book or portions thereof in any form : Published simultane-
ously in Canada by Holt, Rinehart and Winston of Canada, Limited :
Library of Congress Catalog Card Number : AC 67–10230 : Printed
in the United States of America : 92747–0717 : First Edition

To L. B. III

The very first explorers of America were Indians.

When the Pilgrims explored the New England Coast, they found Indians living in small villages of wigwams. This was in 1620.

But explorers from Spain had already discovered the Mexican Indians living in the most beautiful cities they had ever seen.

No one knows exactly how many years
ago the first Indians began to explore the
Americas. Some men say ten thousand
years ago. Others say twenty-five thousand.

But men think they know how the first
Indians came to America. They probably
crossed an ice or land bridge from Asia
to Alaska during the long ice age.

These first Indians were hunters. They carried spears and stones to kill the mammoths, bison, and giant wolves.

Across the land bridge ran the animals. Across the bridge followed the hunters.

Many of these early hunters stayed in Alaska to build homes of ice and snow. We now call these arctic settlers Eskimos.

Other Indians kept moving south. Some of these explorers from Asia settled in the plains, in the deserts, and in the woodlands of what is now the United States.

Still other tribes found their way to Mexico. Some of them even traveled by foot to the tip of South America.

Some of the early Mexican Indians lived in rock caves. Others built mud huts with thatched roofs.

Like all Indians in North America, the Indians of Mexico found wild plants to eat.

After many years, they began planting the seeds of the best tasting foods. In this way they became farmers as well as hunters.

The plant all Indians grew was a kind of corn called maize.

The first Mexican corn cobs were no longer than a strawberry. Only one cob grew on a plant. The kernels were tiny and as hard as our pop corn.

The Indians learned to use only the best kernels for planting. In this way, each corn crop was better than the last.

The Mexican Indians also planted the seeds of squash, beans, and chili-peppers.

Like other Indians, the Indians of Mexico used stones to grind the kernels of corn into a soft meal.

They mixed the meal with water and baked flat corn cakes on flat stones over an open fire.

The early Mexican Indians wove baskets from strips of bark. These were used to hold the ears of corn and other vegetables.

They molded clay pottery bowls. Sometimes they painted a white design on the red clay bowls.

These early Mexican Indians made tiny clay figures that looked like dolls. But they were not dolls. They were images of their gods and goddesses. One was the god of fire. Another was the goddess of corn.

They built altars to their gods on a mound of earth. A few steps led to the altar.

There the Indians could pray to the gods for a good crop of corn.

There came a time when the first Indians of Mexico had to leave their villages. The soil no longer grew strong plants.

Floods covered the old villages with water and dirt. Sometimes a volcano erupted, covering the villages with lava.

These first Indian hunters and farmers left no books or writing. We do not know the names of their tribes or the language they spoke. Only by digging in the buried villages do men know how these Indians lived.

We do have names for later tribes who came from the North in the years between the first Indians and the Aztecs. Some of these Indians built cities on top of the soil that buried the old villages.

One of these tribes was the Olmec. They settled in the jungles along the East Coast of Mexico. Here they found rubber and cocoa trees, jaguars, and brightly colored birds. They also found jade rock.

Some say the Olmecs invented the rubber ball used in the Indian ball game.

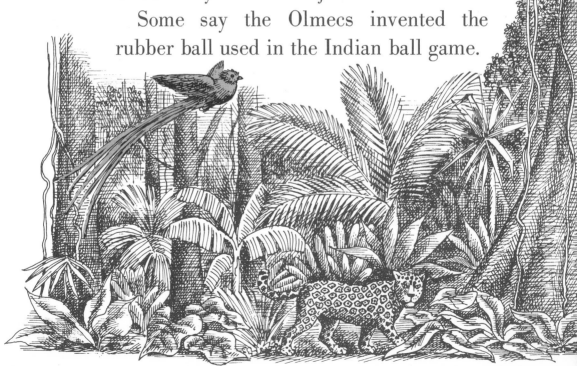

The old Olmec Indians told their children stories about cruel giants who lived on the land before them.

The first Olmecs put the giants to sleep with a sweet drink. Then the Olmecs killed the giants and became rulers of the land.

Perhaps that is why the Olmecs were called the Magicians.

Perhaps that is why the Olmecs carved giant stone heads wherever they lived.

Many other Indian tribes were exploring Mexico at about the same time.

Some of the Maya Indians were probably living in Southern Mexico before the Olmecs arrived there.

The Toltecs built their first great cities in the Valley of Mexico, not far from where Mexico City is today. Later, they, too, moved to the South. There were many tales about one of the Toltec rulers. Some of the stories may be true.

This great ruler was Quetzalcoatl, the Feathered Serpent. He was named for the beautiful quetzal bird and coatl, the serpent.

Quetzalcoatl did not look like an Indian. He had pale skin and he had a beard.

Quetzalcoatl taught his Indians to make books from the bark of trees and from deer skins. These books opened and folded like a screen. In the books the Indians painted tiny picture stories of their history.

Before the time of Quetzalcoatl, the Indians of Mexico tried to please their gods by sacrificing or killing men. The Indians believed the gods would bring sun and rain in return for the lives of the men. They thought the god of war would help them win battles.

Not so, Quetzalcoatl. This good king told the people that the gods were not pleased to have men sacrificed at their altars.

At the end of his life, Quetzalcoatl sailed out to sea in a canoe. But before he left his Toltec Indians, he promised one day to return.

All Indians of Mexico worshipped Quetzalcoatl as a god. They built temples in his honor. They watched for his return.

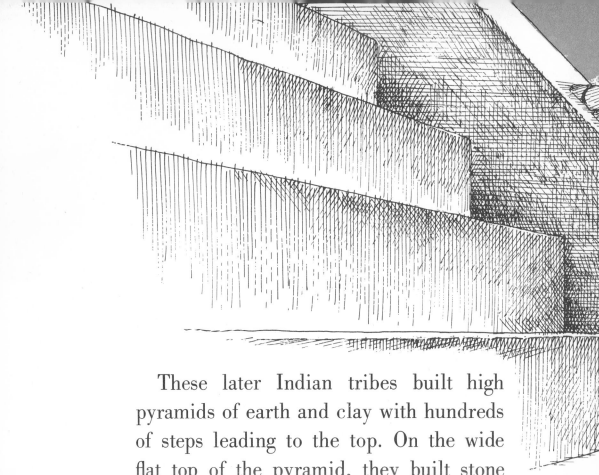

These later Indian tribes built high pyramids of earth and clay with hundreds of steps leading to the top. On the wide flat top of the pyramid, they built stone temples. On the temple walls, they carved designs of their feathered serpent and jaguar gods.

Like the first Indians, the Olmecs, the Maya, and the Toltecs worshipped a corn goddess and a fire god but they had many other gods and goddesses.

On stone monuments, they carved images of their rain gods and rain dwarfs, their sun and moon gods. To keep themselves from harm, the Indians carved ugly masks on their temples and monuments.

On other monuments, they carved kings, warriors, dancers, ball players, and wrestlers.

As did the first Indians, these later ones modeled pottery bowls and figurines. Some of the figurines were pretty ladies, children with laughing faces, fat babies, and hairless dogs.

The Aztecs were the last of the great Indian tribes to arrive from the North. They settled in the Valley of Mexico more than a hundred years before Columbus found America.

It is said that Indian wisemen told the Aztec leaders to search for a certain sign. The sign was to be a live eagle perched on a cactus which grew from a rock. The eagle would hold a serpent in its claw.

At last the Aztecs did find such an eagle. This was their place to settle.

Not far from this spot was the old city built by the Toltecs. Now it was in ruins.

In the distance, the first Aztecs saw rolling hills and two snow covered volcanoes. But their home was to be in the middle of a swamp with lakes on every side.

How could the Aztec explorers build their huts or grow crops in the middle of a swamp?

How were they able to build their beautiful cities of polished stone? How did they ever decorate a palace with silver and gold and fill it with jewels?

These first Aztecs started with nothing but courage and cleverness.

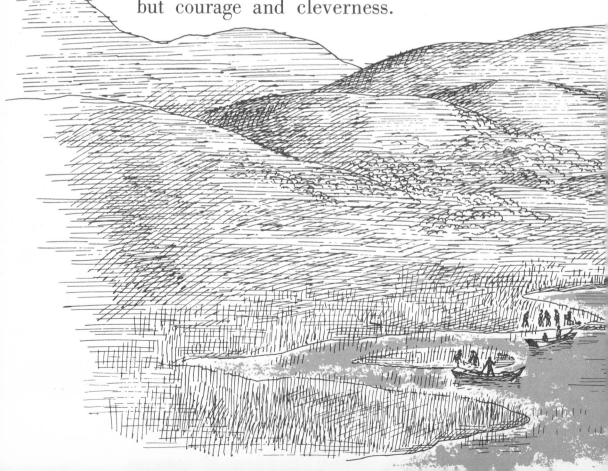

Stories say the Aztecs began their cities by building rafts. Upon these rafts, they piled mud from the swamps. They could then grow gardens on the raft islands. In a few years the roots of the plants grew long enough to reach the bottom of the swamp. There the roots anchored the rafts.

With many rafts anchored together there was solid ground for building. Now the Aztecs needed building materials.

The Aztecs carried fish, eels, frogs, and wild ducks from their swamps to neighboring tribes who lived on dry land. They traded these foods for lumber and building stone.

On the spot where they first saw the eagle, the Aztecs built a temple to their god of war. They dug canals and made canoes to use on them. They built bridges between the islands. They built adobe houses.

The Aztecs were the greatest warriors of all the Indians in Mexico.

When they needed more land they seized it from neighboring tribes. Carrying bows, arrows, lances, and spiked clubs, they went to battle.

For armor they wore padded cotton suits, and wooden shields. On their heads the warriors wore wooden helmets decorated with feathers. The helmets were carved to look like the heads of serpents and tigers. Beating drums, whistling, and screeching, they tried to frighten their neighbors. And they did.

After a hundred years or more, the Aztecs had seized all the land they needed. They were the ruling tribe.

They built a great stone palace for their king. Next to the palace was a court for playing ball games. There was a zoo and an aviary for every kind of bird to be found in Mexico. Orchards of fruit trees and gardens of roses were planted. Ducks, geese, and fish swam in the lakes.

One great temple pyramid loomed over the palace square. There were many smaller temples throughout the city.

Some Indians of other tribes were left to live on the land that now belonged to the Aztecs. These Indians had to pay tribute or taxes to the Aztec king.

From miles around, the conquered Indians brought gold, jade, turquoise, and emeralds to the palace.

They brought bundles of corn and bags of cocoa beans. They brought quetzal bird feathers, embroidered blouses and bundles of paper.

At the palace, Aztec clerks drew pictures of the tribute. By reading these pictures, the king knew which people had paid their taxes.

Rich Aztecs built their houses of stone. They polished the walls so that they shone like silver. They planted flowers in their court yards and on the flat roofs.

Other houses were made of mud bricks painted with white lime.

Each house had two doors. One door led to the street. The other door led to a canal. At the canal door was a canoe.

There were low chairs in some of the houses, but all Indians slept on straw mats. They all cooked on a hearth-stone.

Rich Aztec women dressed in blouses and skirts embroidered in bright colors. The men wore embroidered cloaks.

Both men and women wore bright plumes in their hair. They wore necklaces and earrings set with jewels. On their arms and ankles they wore bracelets. So did the children.

But only the men wore nose ornaments. Only an important man carried a bunch of flowers in his hand when he went on the street.

Not all the Aztecs were rich. Some of them were workers in the city or on the farms.

Like the early Indians, they lived in one room mud huts with thatched roofs.

These workers wore plain white robes and loin cloths. Instead of wearing sandals, they went barefoot.

All Indians met at the market place. Here they could buy, sell, or trade everything they needed.

The Aztecs used cocoa beans for money. If a man had enough cocoa beans, he could even buy an Indian slave at the market.

If there were still more cocoa beans at home, his wife could make a sweet chocolate drink for her family.

Like all Indians, the Aztecs were happy to have children in their family. They called a new baby "Quetzal Feather", or "Precious Jade". They gave feasts and made long speeches of welcome to the baby.

A baby girl was given the present of a little spindle. A baby boy was given a toy shield or a bow with four arrows.

As the children grew older, the mother baked them small cakes to eat at each meal.

Aztec farmers taught their sons to plant corn and beans, and to raise turkeys for the market.

Craftsmen taught their sons to make fine jewelry and feather headdresses.

But some of the Aztecs sent their children to live in one of the temple schools. Priests and warriors were the teachers.

Boys who went to one kind of school learned to be rulers, priests and wisemen. This school was called the Calmecac.

Boys who attended the Calmecac school had little time for rest and play.

They learned to read Indian history from the folding books of picture writing. They learned the holy songs of their people. They were taught to write and speak well, and to count by the Aztec system of numbers.

The priests taught these boys to predict coming events by studying the stars and the Aztec calendar stone.

On cold nights, the Calmecac boys were sent without food to the mountains to pray. So that they would be brave men, the boys scratched their arms and legs with thorns.

The other school for boys was called the Telpochalli. Here boys trained to be warriors.

These boys had an easier life than the Calmecacs. In the daytime, they swept the temple, gathered wood, planted corn, and repaired ditches. The warriors taught them to battle with clubs and to throw spears.

But after sunset, they sang, danced, and talked with their warrior teachers.

Sometimes the Telpochalli boys practiced fighting with the Calmecac boys. Quite often the brave Calmecacs beat the warriors at their own game of war.

Aztec girls attended another temple school. Here priestesses taught the girls to spin and embroider. The girls learned to burn incense to the gods and goddesses.

These girls lived in the temple until they married. Some girls became priestesses and lived at the temple for the rest of their lives.

All Indians enjoyed watching the ball game. Players tried to hit a heavy ball through the hoops on the walls of the ball court. But the players were not allowed to touch the ball with their hands. They had to use their knees, their hips, or elbows.

The audience sat on top of the ball court wall. If a player hit the ball through a hoop, the people tossed him gifts of clothing and jewels as a reward.

The Aztecs had eighteen months on their round calendar. Each month had twenty days.

And each month a feast was celebrated to honor one of the gods. Jugglers and acrobats entertained the crowds. Musicians played drums, gongs, flutes, and trumpets.

At sunset, songs and dances began. Even the ruler joined in some of the dancing. Warriors and women, holding hands, danced between rows of torch bearers. Far into the night, they danced and sang.

Then came the sacrifices.

The Aztecs no longer needed land. But they still went to war to bring home captives. They thought the gods would be pleased to have the captives killed at their altars.

The Aztecs had long ago forgotten the teachings of the good Quetzalcoatl. But they had not forgotten the promise of Quetzalcoatl to return to earth. Wisemen predicted his return in the year of 1519.

One day in the year 1519, an Indian runner asked to see the Aztec ruler, Montezuma.

In his hand the runner held a piece of paper. On the paper were pictures of a ship, men in clothing strange to the Indians, and horses never before seen by an Indian.

The leader of these strangers had fair skin and he wore a beard. Could this be Quetzalcoatl, now a god, come back to earth?

Montezuma was frightened. But he sent an invitation to these strange men to visit in his palace.

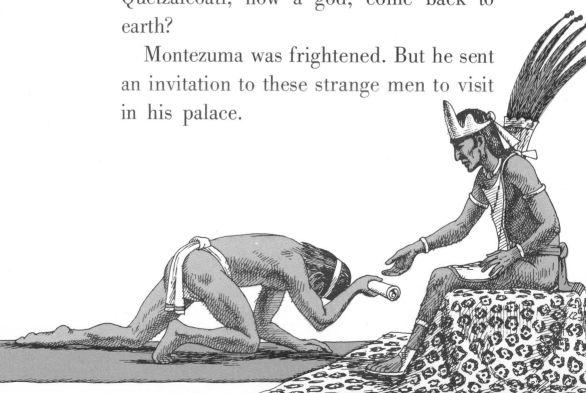

Into the Aztec city rode the strangers on their strange animals. The man with the beard was not the Indian god, Quetzalcoatl. He was Cortez, come from Spain to conquer the Indians.

Cortez was amazed by the beauty of the Aztec cities. But soon the cities were on fire. Indians who first shot arrows at the strangers screamed with fright as they fell under the guns of Cortez and his men.

The Aztec kingdom was in ruins. Cortez had captured for his own king all the riches of the Aztec people.

Only a few of the thousands of books written by the Aztecs were saved from the fires.

Today you can find some Aztec treasures in museums. There are images of the gods and carved stone monuments.

There are spears and arrows, painted shields, helmets, and drums once carried by the warriors.

There are a few pieces of jewelry and feathered headdresses worn at one time by the proud Aztec people.

Men are still digging for buried books and treasures so that we may learn more about the history of the Mexican Indians.

But, best of all, men are trying to rebuild some of those beautiful temples and palaces. Someday we may see for ourselves the wonderful world of the Mexican Indian.

MARGARET C. FARQUHAR has been interested in books since she was very young when, with several friends, she organized the Oz Club with the purpose of dramatizing the books of Frank Baum. Now a library consultant for elementary and junior high schools, her experience enables her to evaluate the interests and needs of children in regard to books. *The Indians of Mexico* stemmed from a trip to Mexico which convinced her that younger children who were fascinated with the American Indians would be intrigued to learn of those who had found their way to Mexico. Mrs. Farquhar holds a B.A. from the University of Michigan, an M.S. in education from Teacher's College of Columbia University, and an M.S. in library science from Western Reserve University.

MEL KLAPHOLZ studied commercial art at the Newark School of Fine and Industrial Art and figure drawing at the Art Students' League. A free-lance illustrator of books and magazines, he has also exhibited paintings in several galleries and national exhibitions. Normally a resident of Pennsylvania, Mr. Klapholz gained a first-hand acquaintance with Mexico during a ten-month stay in San Miguel DeAllende, an old Colonial town in the mountains of Mexico.

About the book: The title is set in Beton Medium Condensed capitals and the text type face is Bodoni Book. The book was printed by offset. The carefully researched illustrations are pen and ink line drawings printed in brown with blue wash inside and black pen and ink line with brown and blue washes on the jacket. Mr. Klapholz used a sponge to apply paint where texture was desired.